SKYDIVING

Diane Bailey

Rourke
Educational Media
rourkeeducationalmedia.com

*Scan for Related Titles
and Teacher Resources*

Before Reading:

Building Academic Vocabulary and Background Knowledge

Before reading a book, it is important to tap into what your child or students already know about the topic. This will help them develop their vocabulary, increase their reading comprehension, and make connections across the curriculum.

1. *Look at the cover of the book. What will this book be about?*
2. *What do you already know about the topic?*
3. *Let's study the Table of Contents. What will you learn about in the book's chapters?*
4. *What would you like to learn about this topic? Do you think you might learn about it from this book? Why or why not?*
5. *Use a reading journal to write about your knowledge of this topic. Record what you already know about the topic and what you hope to learn about the topic.*
6. *Read the book.*
7. *In your reading journal, record what you learned about the topic and your response to the book.*
8. *After reading the book complete the activities below.*

Content Area Vocabulary
Read the list. What do these words mean?

acrobatics
altimeter
altitude
antenna
canopy
descent
freefall
paratroopers
rectangular
rigger
right-of-way
ripcord
synchronized
tracking

After Reading:

Comprehension and Extension Activity

After reading the book, work on the following questions with your child or students in order to check their level of reading comprehension and content mastery.

1. *How does the parachute design affect the skydiver? (Asking questions)*
2. *Explain how the de-arch position and head-down position work with air to make a diver go slower or faster. (Visualize)*
3. *What are the similarities and differences between a parachute and a wingsuit? (Summarize)*
4. *How do divers steer their body when falling? (Summarize)*
5. *Would you go skydiving? Explain. (Text to self connection)*

Extension Activity

Skydivers rely heavily on their parachutes. A diver needs a chute that creates resistance and allows a slow fall to the ground. Design a parachute by using a plastic bag, scissors, string, and a small object to act as the diver, such as an action figure or plastic army man. Cut out a large square from the plastic bag. Trim the square into a design you think would work best. Cut a small hole near the edge of each side and thread the string through the holes. Attach the string to the object you chose as the diver. Using a chair or another high spot, drop your parachute. Did it fall quickly or slowly? Did it tangle? Remember you want it to fall slowly. Make adjustments to your parachute as needed and test again.

TABLE OF CONTENTS

INTO THE SKY!

Nancy Koreen felt a little nervous. No wonder—she was about to jump out of a plane! Nancy had skydived many times, but this time was special. She was part of a team of women preparing to do a group skydive. There were 63 of them all together, in three different planes.

In a few moments, the doors of the planes would open and the women would jump. Then they would try to join hands as they dove down at 160 miles (257.5 kilometers) per hour. If they did it, they would set a world record in skydiving. To succeed, everyone had to be perfectly **synchronized** at the same time. They had less than a minute to get it right.

The door opened and the howling wind hit Nancy's body. It was loud and cold. She didn't care, though. The clock was ticking. It was time to make history! She took a deep breath, and jumped into the sky.

GETTING STARTED

Andre-Jacques Garnerin (1769–1823)

In the late 1700s, Andre-Jacques Garnerin did not have much to do. He had been captured during the French Revolution. Now he was stuck in prison. To pass the time, he dreamed of making a parachute. In 1797, after he got out of prison, he set to work. He made a parachute out of a big piece of white canvas, more than 20 feet (6 meters) across. Then he attached a basket to it. He rode in a balloon to take him high above the ground, and took his parachute with

him. When he reached 3,200 feet (975 meters), he floated down in a basket as the parachute opened above him. People liked this new way of flying. They used balloons to parachute all through the 1800s. A new sport was born!

Inspired

Leonardo da Vinci was a famous artist and scientist in the 1400s. He drew a sketch of a parachute, but never built it. In 2000, a skydiver named Adrian Nichols decided he would make da Vinci's parachute. It was made from canvas, wooden poles, and rope. Then Nichols tested it. It worked!

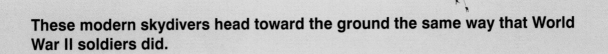

These modern skydivers head toward the ground the same way that World War II soldiers did.

Airplanes were invented in the 1900s. They flew higher and faster than balloons did. Airplane shows were popular in the 1920s. Parachutes were part of the entertainment. Crowds loved to watch them. World War II started in 1939. There was a new use for parachutes. Soldiers used them to jump out of airplanes. They flew directly into battle zones. These **paratroopers** helped win the war.

The war ended in 1945. Soldiers did not need parachutes anymore. There were still a lot of them laying around! Some people decided to parachute just for fun. In the 1950s, the jumper Raymond Young gave the sport a new name. He called it skydiving. Through the 1960s and 1970s, schools opened to teach skydiving. People held competitions. Parachutes got better and safer. More people tried it. Today, there is a group called the United States Parachute Association (USPA). It estimated that skydivers made more than three million jumps in 2014. That's a lot of air time!

Today's parachutes are more like wide wings than round-topped bags.

Surf's Up

The surf is way up in skysurfing—way up in the air! Skysurfers attach a board to their feet. It is shaped like a surfboard, but is smaller. As the skydivers fall, they catch the wind just like surfers catch waves.

Imagine being able to dance or do gymnastics in the air. Skydivers have about a minute before they open their parachutes. This **freefall** is when they get to play in the sky! They can do **acrobatics** such as loops, flips, and turns. Two or more skydivers can dance with each other in a midair ballet.

Skydiving in groups is also popular. Divers hold on to each other's arms and legs to make shapes such as circles or stars. This is called formation skydiving. There can be hundreds of people in one dive. That requires a lot of planning and good timing.

Speed skydiving started in the mid-2000s. These divers go as fast as they can. They can reach speeds of more than 300 miles (482.8 kilometers) per hour.

Skydivers can link up together during the freefall part of their jump.

Skydiving starts on the ground. Divers practice their moves over and over. How will they move their body? How will they pull the **ripcord** to open the parachute? This trains their muscles to remember what to do. It helps prevent making a mistake in the air.

For their first jump, skydivers often ride piggyback with a skydiving teacher. The teacher makes sure they stay safe,

Carefully packed parachutes are lined up before skydivers head into the air.

First-time skydivers often are linked together with an instructor.

so the student can focus on learning and having fun. New students can jump alone by using a special cord. One end of the cord is hooked to the plane. The other end attaches to the jumper's parachute. The cord automatically releases the parachute at the right time. Some students want to jump with a teacher beside them. This type of jump starts higher, and allows more time to practice freefall. After enough jumps, students can skydive on their own.

SPORTS SKILLS

After checking the weather, it's time to leave the airplane!

How's the weather? That is the first question a skydiver asks. Strong winds might blow them off course. They cannot jump into clouds, because they must always be able to see around them. Even rain can hurt. At high speeds, raindrops feel like needles pricking the skin.

Skydives can start anywhere from about 3,500 to 15,000 feet (1,057 to 4,572 meters) above the ground. Higher jumps give skydivers more time in freefall. Jumps with a lot of people start higher. They need more time to get organized.

Skydivers also must plan where to land. This is their drop zone. A spotter guides the plane's pilot to exactly the right place to let the skydivers out. Spotters are trained to look straight down. That's harder than it sounds! Spotters also check the speed and

Spotters and other jumpers check the ground carefully before they make any jump.

direction of the wind. They look for possible obstacles on the ground, such as trees, water, or power lines. They make sure there are no other skydivers too close.

Even while falling, skydivers feel like they are floating on air.

Skydivers do not open their parachutes right away. First, they fly! Freefall lasts about a minute. It can be longer or shorter depending on the beginning **altitude** of the jump. Skydivers are too high to see any objects on the ground, so they do not feel like they are falling. Instead they feel like they are floating on a pillow of air, even though they are going very fast. Divers reach their top speed in just a few seconds. It is usually about 120 miles (193 kilometers) per hour. At that speed, they fall the height of a 16-story building every second. Speed skydivers go even faster.

Moving that fast can be dangerous. Skydivers can hit each other in mid-air. Fortunately, there are some traffic rules to help out. The **right-of-way** in skydiver traffic goes to the diver who is lowest. Divers pass each other on the right.

Skydivers must move carefully when they are not alone in the sky.

By spreading their arms and legs, skydivers can change how fast they are falling.

How do airplanes stay in the sky? They make the wind work for them. Planes are designed so that the flow of air around them helps lift them up. Skydivers do the same thing. They can move their bodies so they go faster, slower, or sideways.

Sometimes there is more than one skydiver at the same level in the air. They must be sure to keep enough distance between them. They can move away from each other by **tracking**. To do this, they straighten their bodies a little and make a slight arch. This changes how the air moves around their bodies and pushes them sideways. If more of their body hits the wind, it slows them down. If they want to turn, they tilt their arms in the direction they want to go. Their arms work like an airplane's wings. That is why skydivers call themselves body pilots.

Arching or twisting their bodies helps skydivers steer.

IN POSITION

Skydivers need to choose the right body position. This helps them turn, move sideways, and go faster or slower. Here are some of the body positions they can choose.

Belly-to-Earth or "Box Man": The skydiver faces down in this basic freefall position. The legs are bent about halfway at the knees and the arms are bent at the elbows to make a U-shape. The back sinks down a little, so the hips are at the lowest point.

De-Arch: To slow down, skydivers can reverse their position a little. They arch their back toward the sky, instead of to the ground. Imagine hugging a huge beach ball. The "ball" of air lifts the body.

Head-Down: In this position, the arms are straight back, close to the body. The head is pointing to the ground. The diver looks like a human bullet—and moves like one, too! This position gives divers a lot of speed.

Skydivers keep a close eye on their **altimeter** as they fall. This device measures their altitude, which is how many

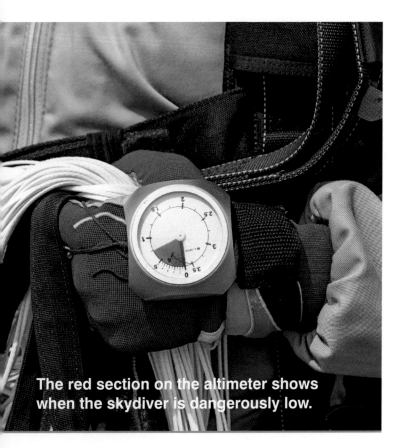

The red section on the altimeter shows when the skydiver is dangerously low.

feet they are above the ground. At about 3,500 feet (1,067 meters), it is time to pull the ripcord. This releases the parachute. A small pilot chute opens first. It is only a few feet across. The pilot chute pulls the main parachute into position. The **canopy** opens up and slows the skydiver down to about 10 miles (16 kilometers) per hour.

Steering handles on modern chutes make it easier to have soft landings.

Skydivers steer by pulling cords attached to the parachute. There are two handles—one on the right and one on the left. Pulling on both of them at the same time brakes the parachute and slows their **descent**.

What happens if the parachute does not open? That is rare. Just in case, all parachute packs come with a backup. The reserve parachute works just like the main one. The parachute also has an automatic device that will open it if the skydiver does not.

Coming in for a landing should be as easy as taking a little jog.

Prepare for landing! Skydivers steer the parachute to their drop zone. At about 15 feet (4.6 meters) above the ground, they start to pull both steering lines. This brakes the parachute. It gives them a little bit of last-minute lift. Most landings are only about as hard as jumping off a low wall. If things do get bumpy, divers take most of the impact on the balls of their feet. Then they roll into the fall. This transfers the force up the side of their body.

Indoor Skydiving

If skydivers want to get in some extra air time, they can go indoor skydiving. For this, they go to a vertical wind tunnel. Powerful machines blow air in a long column and skydivers can float on it. They feel like they are in freefall, even though they may only be a few feet off the ground. It gives them a chance to practice their moves.

GEAR UP

The scoops at the front edge of this parachute help the skydiver steer.

A parachute may be round or **rectangular** in shape. Most skydivers prefer the rectangular ones. They are easier to steer. Rectangular chutes have two layers of fabric. The back and sides are sewn shut, while the front is open. There are also ribs inside the canopy that divide it into smaller sections. They are called ram-air canopies because air flows, or rams, into the canopy from the front. The sections fill with air and make the canopy stiff, like an airplane wing. Using this type of chute, skydivers can steer exactly where they want to go.

In the past, parachutes were made of silk or canvas. Today, most are made from nylon. It is lightweight and flexible. It resists the wind well and takes a long time to wear out. Most of all, it is strong. Nylon parachutes use extra-thick thread. They are woven using a design of small squares. If the parachute rips, this pattern stops the tear from spreading too far.

Thin, but strong: In any color, parachute fabric gets the job done.

Only experts should roll and pack a parachute before a jump.

A parachute is packed inside a special backpack called a container system. Skydivers wear a harness that holds it in place. It wraps around their arms and legs so it can't fall off. Parachute canopies range from about 100 to 200 square feet (9.2 to 18.5 square meters). That means the short side of a parachute can be taller than the ceiling of a normal room. The long side is more than twice as long. There are also dozens of strings and cords that keep it in place. That is a lot of parachute to fit inside a small backpack. Skydivers can't just stuff it all in!

Parachutes must be folded in certain places. They must be packed into the backpack in a specific way. The lines must be laid so that they will not twist or get tangled up. Some packing is done on a table. Other times, skydivers work on their hands and knees, folding. A parachute **rigger** is trained to pack parachutes correctly. Riggers can also repair parachutes if they get ripped or damaged.

Shoulder and leg straps hold the pack to the jumper's body.

Skydivers carry a lot of gear—about 30 pounds (13 kilograms) of it! Every piece helps them stay safe and comfortable. Most skydivers wear goggles or sunglasses to shield their eyes from the wind. Helmets protect their heads in

Helmets with face shields provide protection from wind—and crashes.

case they bump into each other or have a rocky landing. Some people like to feel the wind on their face. They choose helmets that do not have face masks. People flying in teams usually wear helmets with face masks. Those offer crash protection, too.

Most skydivers wear a special jumpsuit. It is one piece and zips up neatly. There is nothing flapping around to get in the way. Some jumpsuits fit tightly and are made of slippery fabric. These help the skydiver go faster. There are also suits that fit more loosely and are made of rougher material, such as canvas. These slow divers down. They are good for heavier people.

WIth the jump over, it's time to haul the parachute back to the packing shed.

Flying Squirrels

Maybe the first wingsuit flyers got the idea from another animal: flying squirrels. Folds of skin stretch between their legs. This helps them glide through the air as they jump from tree to tree.

To stay in the air even longer, skydivers can wear a wingsuit. Wingsuits have sheets of fabric that stretch between the diver's wrists, armpits, and hips. Another piece stretches between the legs. Small, open spaces are sewn into the fabric. They puff up as they catch the air and make the suit stiff. Now, the skydiver has been turned into a human wing! Wingsuits help skydivers move sideways through the air. They can glide more slowly.

People tried early versions of wingsuits more than 100 years ago. The French tailor Franz Reichelt made one in 1912. Then he jumped off the Eiffel Tower. Unfortunately, the fabric did

The wingsuit spreads out to to allow the skydiver to ride the wind.

not spread out properly. He died in the fall. Since then, wingsuits have gotten much better. Wingsuit flyers still use parachutes to slow them down for a safe landing.

THE STARS

kydivers are always trying more. They want to fly faster, stay up longer, and do extreme moves. Meet some skydivers who are flying high!

Luigi Cani is one of the world's most successful skydivers.

LUIGI CANI

Luigi Cani likes to set records! Luigi is from Brazil and has won 79 medals in skydiving. He set a record for the fastest freefall speed. He flew 343 miles (552 kilometers) per hour! He has also landed while using the smallest parachute. Luigi has jumped more than 11,000 times. He has turned his love for skydiving into a career. He is a test pilot for new parachutes, and makes movies about skydiving.

AMY CHMELECKI

Amy Chmelecki is one of the best-known women in skydiving. She made her first jump when she was 18. After that, she never looked back. Amy is from New York and moved to Arizona after college to practice skydiving. Soon she decided to make it her career. She has jumped about 13,000 times and has won many contests. Amy is part of an all-women team of skydivers called the Joy Riders.

Amy Chmelecki often wears a wingsuit for her jumps.

BASE Jumpers

Go jump off a bridge! No, really. That is one of the things BASE jumpers do. Instead of jumping out of a plane, they jump from tall objects. BASE stands for Building, **Antenna**, Span (a bridge), and Earth. BASE jumpers have jumped from the Petronas Towers in Malaysia, photo at right, and from the top of Mt. Everest. That's the tallest mountain in the world. BASE jumping is very risky. The altitudes are usually lower than skydives, so jumpers have less time to open their parachutes.

LUKE AIKINS

Luke Aikins comes from a family of skydivers. His parents and grandparents did it, too! Luke made his first jump in 1989. Since then he has jumped 15,000 times. Luke works as a professional skydiver. He does shows and teaches skydiving. He has also won several medals. Luke grew up in Washington. One of his favorite events was jumping into the football stadium of the Seattle Seahawks, to deliver the game ball.

Luke Aikins uses his jumping skills to record other jumpers with a helmet camera.

Skydivers get great views of rivers, fields, cities, and more as they look for a good place to land.

Oceans or deserts? Mountains or rainforests? Skydivers get the best views there are. They can choose from all the world's amazing scenery. There are also some challenging routes to take. Valery Rozov is a skydiver from Russia. He flew into an active volcano in Russia. He did not get too hot, though! The mountains there are cold enough that the volcano had ice inside. Instead of lava, Valery landed on the ice.

In 1960, United States Air Force pilot Joe Kittinger set a skydiving record. He jumped from space —19 miles (30.5

kilometers) above Earth! In 2012, Austrian skydiver Felix Baumgartner broke that record. He jumped from 24 miles (38.6 kilometers) up. Felix reached a speed of more than 800 miles (1,287 kilometers) per hour during his freefall. That is faster than the speed of sound. He reached the ground in less than ten minutes. Felix's altitude record was broken in 2014 by American Alan Eustace. He went up to 25 miles (40.2 kilometers).

Felix Baumgartner was nearly in space when he began his record jump.

Landing on a target is part of many skydiving competitions.

Imagine falling through the air for a mile, doing loops and turns the whole way. Now, straighten up, open your parachute, and steer for the landing spot. Look close—it is a disk only the size of a quarter! That is what skydiving competition is like.

Skydivers like to compete to see who is best at certain things. Who is fastest? Who has the best moves? Who can stay up the longest? Skydivers often compete as teams, with four or eight people. They work to make certain formations in the air—and they only have a little time to get it right. One competition is for canopy pilots. Pilots are good at steering their parachutes. They can swoop through narrow, difficult courses. They are judged on their speed, distance, and accuracy.

Competitions are held all over the world. One is in the city of Dubai, in the Middle East. About five hundred people take part. The teams are from some 25 different countries around the world.

Group skydivers learn safe and quick ways to link up as they fall to the ground.

BACK TO EARTH!

Nancy Koreen hoped that she and her teammates could set a skydiving record. For their jump, 63 women would fly upside-down, hands joined, zooming toward Earth at 160 miles (257.5 kilometers) per hour. If they succeeded, they would be largest all-women group ever to fly together in that position.

Nancy practiced on the ground first. She went through her moves again and again. She knew exactly what to do. Still, it was easy to make a mistake flying that fast. What if she moved her leg

The team takes to the sky to attempt a world record jump.

just two inches too far? That could send her off track. If even one person was not in the right place, the formation would not work. Then they would have to start all over again. Nancy did not want to be the one who messed up!

Even with practice, big jumps with a lot of people do not usually work the first time. The women had already jumped ten or more times trying to get it right. Would this time be the charm? Nancy hoped so!

Nancy jumped from the plane. Seconds counted now. The wind roared in her ears as she found her place. She grabbed the hand of the woman next to her. That woman held on to the next one. One by one they all connected. The feeling was electric. Even through the noise, Nancy could hear everyone yelling and cheering. She knew they had done it!

For a few seconds, they held the position. Then they separated to a safe distance apart and opened their parachutes. As they floated safely to the ground, they grinned and gave each other the thumbs-up sign. That was fun! On the ground, the judges confirmed they had set a record. Now they could start

A cameraman jumps with the team to capture the action.

The record moment: 63 women skydivers link hands and feet in midair!

planning their next jump.

Skydivers love to fly fast and free. They are always looking for the next chance to strap on a parachute and jump into the sky. For a few magical moments, they can ride the wind wherever they want to go.

GLOSSARY

acrobatics (ak-roh-BAT-iks): gymnastic moves like spinning, twisting, or flipping

altimeter (al-TIH-mih-ter): a device that measures altitude

altitude (AL-tih-tood): the height above the ground

antenna (an-TEN-uh): a tall tower that receives communication signals, such as for cell phones

canopy (KAN-up-pea): the fabric part of a parachute

descent (de-SENT): the act of coming down from a high place

freefall (FREE-fall): the time that skydivers fall before opening their parachutes

paratroopers (PARE-uh-troo-pers): soldiers who use a parachute

rectangular (rek-TANG-you-ler): a box-shape with two longer sides and two shorter ones

rigger (RIG-er): a person who packs parachutes into a container system

right-of-way (RITE-of-way): the right to go first in traffic

ripcord (RIP-kord): a rope that skydivers pull to open their parachutes

synchronized (SINK-roh-nized): matched up exactly

tracking (TRAK-ing): moving sideways in the air

INDEX

SHOW WHAT YOU KNOW

1. How were parachutes used during World War II?

2. How fast can speed skydivers go?

3. What are two body positions skydivers use?

4. Why do most skydivers like to use rectangular parachutes?

5. What does a parachute rigger do?

WEBSITES TO VISIT

http://adventure.howstuffworks.com/skydiving.htm

www.uspa.org/AboutSkydiving/tabid/58/Default.aspx

www.dropzone.com

ABOUT THE AUTHOR

Diane Bailey has written about 40 nonfiction books for kids and teens, on topics ranging from science to sports to celebrities. Diane also works as a freelance editor, helping authors who write novels for children and young adults. Diane has two sons, two dogs, and lives in Kansas.

Meet The Author!
www.meetREMauthors.com

© 2016 Rourke Educational Media

www.rourkeeducationalmedia.com

PHOTO CREDITS: Cover © TKTKTKT.
Interior: Niklas Daniel: 42, 43, 44, 45. Dollar Photo: Igor Gromoff 12; Strannik9211 22, 31; Pinosub 24; Freefly 26; Aleksei Lazukov 33. Dreamstime.com: NKoravos 4; Wessel Cirkel 8; Tan Wei Ming 9, title page; Germanskydive 11, 13, 14, 16, 17, 18, 19, 20, 21 bottom; John Morris/Canadian Skyhawks Team Photo 15; Joggie Botman 21top; Melanie Horne 23; Olena Vasylkova 25; Tamas Szoke 28; Deymos 29; Budda 30; Kamonrutm 32; Sérgio Barbará Filho 34; Red Bull Content Pool: 35; Rene Drouyer 36; Temptation 1 38; Dreamframer 40; Joggie Botma 41. Library of Congress: 6, 7. Newscom: Red Bull Stratos 39; Sven Hoffmann/Red Bull/Zuma Press 37.

Edited by: Keli Sipperley
Produced by Shoreline Publishing Group
Design by: Bill Madrid, Madrid Design

Library of Congress PCN Data

Skydiving / Diane Bailey
(Intense Sports)
ISBN 978-1-63430-443-6 (hard cover)
ISBN 978-1-63430-543-3 (soft cover)
ISBN 978-1-63430-631-7 (e-Book)
Library of Congress Control Number: 2015932639
Printed in the United States of America, North Mankato, Minnesota

Also Available as:

ROURKE'S
e-Books